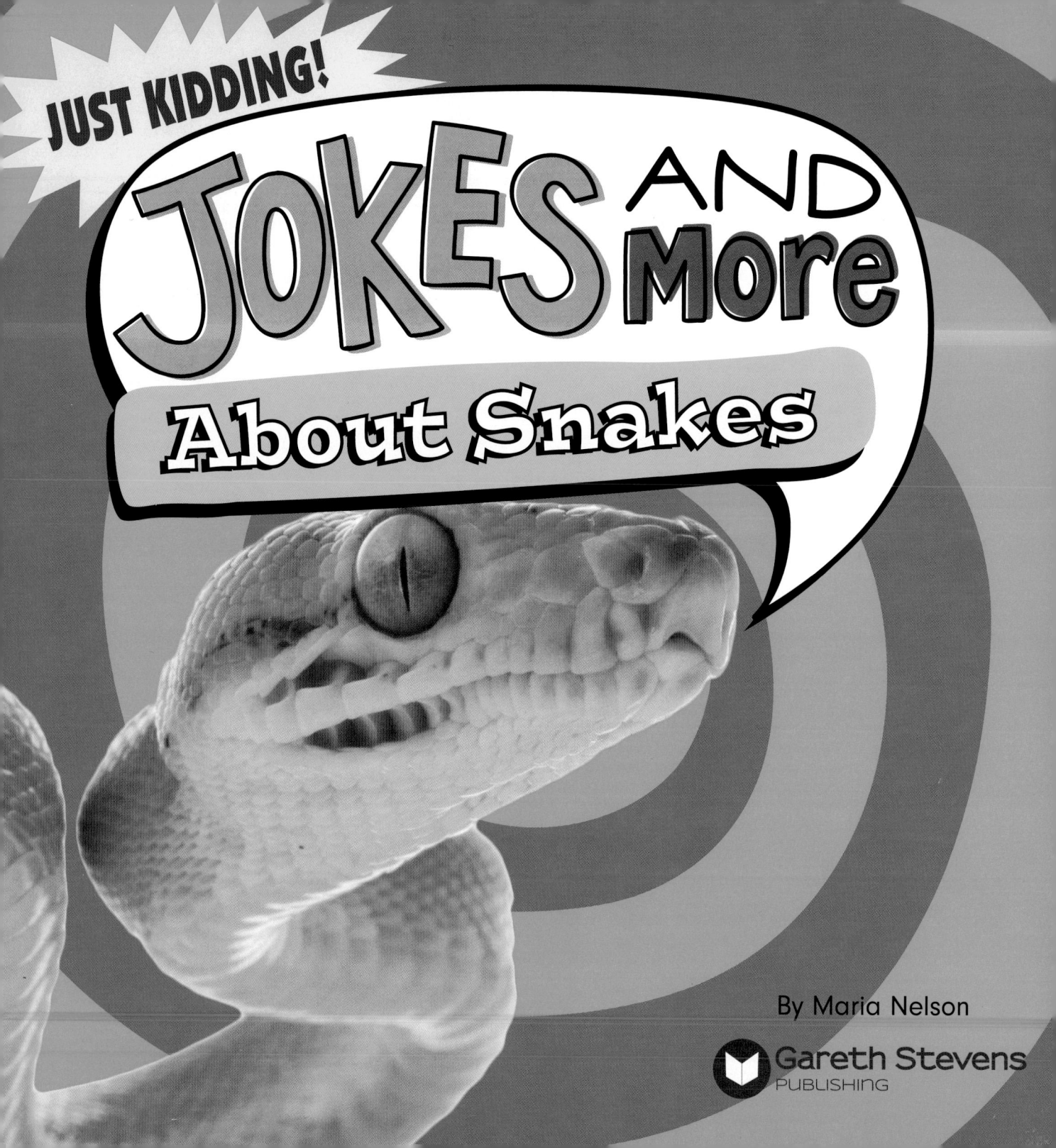

Please visit our website, www.garethstevens.com. For a free color catalog of all our high-quality books, call toll free 1-800-542-2595 or fax 1-877-542-2596.

Library of Congress Cataloging-in-Publication Data

Nelson, Maria.
Jokes and more about snakes / by Maria Nelson.
  p. cm. — (Just kidding!)
Includes index.
ISBN 978-1-4824-0555-2 (pbk.)
ISBN 978-1-4824-0557-6 (6-pack)
ISBN 978-1-4824-0554-5 (library binding)
1. Snakes — Juvenile humor. 2. Wit and humor, Juvenile. I. Nelson, Maria. II. Title.
PN6231.S6 N45 2014
818.5402—dc23

First Edition

Published in 2015 by
Gareth Stevens Publishing
111 East 14th Street, Suite 349
New York, NY 10003

Copyright © 2015 Gareth Stevens Publishing

Designer: Sarah Liddell
Editor: Kristen Rajczak

Photo credits: Cover, p. 1 fivespots/Shutterstock.com; p. 5 Alexandra Lande/Shutterstock.com; pp. 6 (left), 10 (right), 17 (right), 18 (left) dedMazay/Shutterstock.com; pp. 6 (right), 9 (left), 10 (left), 13 (right), 14 (right), 17 (left), 18 (right) Sylverarts/Shutterstock.com; p. 7 Ivan Kuzmin/Shutterstock.com; p. 8 Ryan M. Bolton/Shutterstock.com; pp. 9 (right), 13 (left), 14 (left) Andrey Makurin/ Shutterstock.com; p. 11 KarSol/Shutterstock.com; p. 12 Jason Mintzer/Shutterstock.com; p. 15 pattyphotoart/Shutterstock.com; p. 16 Andre Coetzer/Shutterstock.com; p. 19 Sam DCruz/ Shutterstock.com; p. 20 Simon_g/Shutterstock.com; p. 21 Kaliva/Shutterstock.com; p. 22 (top snake) Dr. Morley Read/Shutterstock.com; p. 22 (bottom snake) JDCarballo/Shutterstock.com.

Printed in the United States of America

CPSIA compliance information: Batch #CS15GS: For further information contact Gareth Stevens, New York, New York at 1-800-542-2595.

Contents

Words in the glossary appear in **bold** type the first time they are used in the text.

Ancient Animal

There are nearly 3,000 **species** of snake. They're found on every continent except Antarctica and have been slithering around Earth since about 130 million years ago!

Snakes are predators that only eat meat. Some kill their **prey** with poisonous bites, such as the cobra and black mamba. Pythons kill their dinner by coiling tightly around it and squeezing until it can't breathe anymore. However, most snakes just swallow their prey whole! Can these creepy creatures be funny? You bet!

What kind of snake keeps its car the cleanest?

A windshield viper.

I've Got the Munchies!

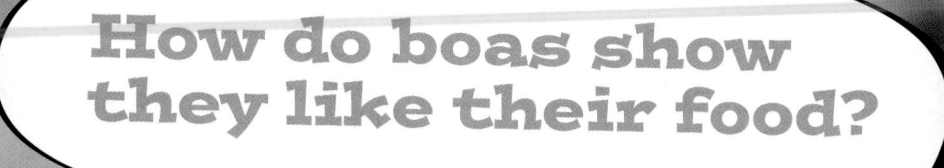

How do boas show they like their food?

They give it a good squeeze.

Sweet Snakes

What do you call a cobra with a great personality?

A snake charmer.

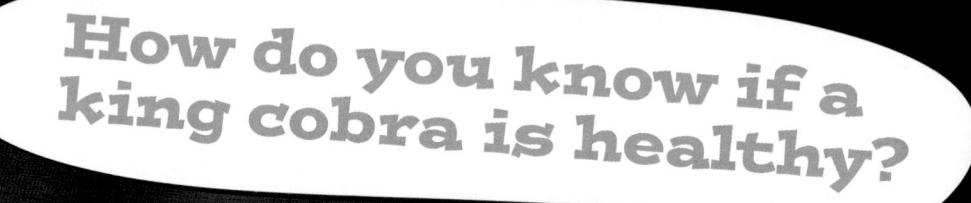

How do you know if a king cobra is healthy?

Check under the hood.

Snake Problems

Two snakes were slithering down the road. One asked the other, "Are we the kind of snake that has a poisonous bite?" The second snake said, "Yes. Why do you ask?"
The first snake looked nervous and exclaimed, "Because I just bit my tongue!"

How do you know if a snake is careless?
Because it keeps losing its skin!

Why did the snake go to the sword store?
He wanted to get some arms.
What's the worst gift a boa constrictor can give?
A hug.

Fun and Funny Facts About Snakes

Not all legless **reptiles** are snakes. Some lizards only have front or back legs or may have no legs at all!

About 375 species of snake are **venomous**. These snakes often have a wide head that swells out behind their eyes. That's where they store the venom!

Snakes can control how much venom is in their bite. Many times when a snake bites a person it's only **defending** itself and so doesn't release any venom. A snake doesn't have an unlimited supply of venom and doesn't want to waste it biting something that it can't eat!

Snakes don't have outer ears like people do, but they do have inner ears that can feel movement in the ground through their jawbone. They use this feeling to "hear." In addition, snakes use their tongues to "smell" the air around them!

defend: to guard against harm

hood: a crest on the head of an animal or an expansion of the head

personality: a creature's nature and ways of acting

prey: an animal that is hunted by other animals for food

reptile: an animal covered with scales or plates that breathes air, has a backbone, and lays eggs, such as a turtle, snake, lizard, or crocodile

serpent: another word for snake

species: a group of plants or animals that are all the same kind

venomous: containing venom, a poison an animal makes in its body

For More Information

BOOKS

Dahl, Michael. *The Funny Farm: Jokes About Dogs, Cats, Ducks, Snakes, Bears, and Other Animals.* Mankato, MN: Picture Window Books, 2011.

Rustad, Martha E. H. *The World's Longest Snake and Other Animal Records.* North Mankato, MN: Capstone Press, 2014.

WEBSITES

Animal Jokes and Riddles
www.enchantedlearning.com/jokes/topics/animal.shtml
Find lots of jokes about all kinds of animals on this website.

Creature Features: Boa Constrictors
kids.nationalgeographic.com/kids/animals/creaturefeature/boa/
Check out facts, videos, and pictures of one of the world's coolest snakes.